First Garden

"No occupation is so delightful to me as the culture of the earth, and no culture comparable to that of the garden." Thomas Jefferson

A Chanticleer Press Edition

First Garden

C.Z. Guest

Introduction by Truman Capote
Drawings by Cecil Beaton
Photographs by Elvin McDonald

Design by Massimo Vignelli

McGraw-Hill Book Company

New York St. Louis San Francisco Auckland
Bogotá Hamburg Johannesburg London
Madrid Milan Mexico Montreal
New Delhi Panama Paris São Paulo
Singapore Sydney Tokyo Toronto

First Printing

ISBN 0-07-025104-5

Library of Congress Cataloging-in-Publication Data
Guest, C.Z.
First garden.
"A Chanticleer Press edition."
Includes index.
1. Gardening. I. Title.
SB453.G88   1987   635
86-20123
ISBN 0-07-025104-5

Portions of the chapter entitled "Flowers" have previously appeared in the June, 1976 issue of *The Ladies' Home Journal*.

Printed and bound by Dai Nippon,
Tokyo, Japan
Typeset by Dix Type Inc., Syracuse,
New York

Chanticleer Staff
Publisher: Paul Steiner
Editor-in-Chief: Gudrun Buettner
Executive Editor: Susan Costello
Managing Editor: Jane Opper
Associate Editor: David Allen
Production: Helga Lose, Gina Stead
Art Associate: Ayn Svoboda

Design: Massimo Vignelli

Contents

Preface

I wrote my book _First Garden_ in 1976.
It doesn't seem possible that it was so long ago,
but fortunately a book like this never goes out of
style. _First Garden_ is a simple garden primer
written for all who want to learn the ABCs of
gardening and have fun doing it. I often find
myself referring back to _First Garden_ for tidbits
of information, and I've received many, many
letters from gardeners who say they still use it
almost like a Bible!
Since the book has been so popular I decided to
bring it up to date, but this time adding a
new dimension—photographs of my own, private
gardens which have never been viewed publicly.
I've been asked numerous times to have the
gardens photographed, but I have never
before allowed it. This change of heart can be
primarily credited to my good garden pal Elvin
McDonald, who is not only a famous gardener
in his own right, cultural affairs director of the
Brooklyn Botanic Garden, but also a top-notch
photographer. Elvin convinced me that my
gardens were too beautiful to keep all to myself,
and his glorious pictures show my gardens the way
I would like you all to see them.
This book is dedicated to the four great passions
in my life, my husband, my children, my horses,
and my gardens.

C.Z. Guest

C.Z. by Truman Capote

Though I've wandered along many a shady lane, and down several primrose paths, I can't pretend to know much about gardening. However, I know quite a lot, more than she might prefer, about the author of the present volume, Mrs. Winston F. C. Guest. Otherwise known as C.Z. Or sometimes Cee-Zee. Actually, her name is Lucy; but the only person who occasionally calls her that is her husband.

The first time I saw Mrs. Guest was during the entr'acte on the opening night of _My Fair Lady_. Escorted by Cecil Beaton, the play's costume-designer, she was standing at a bar across from the theatre. There were fifty-odd fashionable ladies crowded there, but one could not have overlooked this one.

As Raymond Chandler remarked of his femme fatale in _The Long Goodbye_: "There are blondes, and then there are blondes." Mrs. Guest, shimmering in the blue smoky light, was one of the latter. Her hair, parted in the middle and paler than Dom Pérignon, was but a shade darker than the dress she was wearing, a Main Bocher column of white crêpe de chine. No jewelry, not much makeup; just blanc de blanc perfection. Mr. Beaton introduced me to her, a gesture she acknowledged with ice-cream reserve. Who could have imagined that lurking inside this cool vanilla lady was a madcap, laughing tomboy? Well, I suppose anyone who knew her background: a trimly, tautly brought up Boston girl, the

Winter is an important time for plants, a time to rest and store energy for next year. Planted in 1906, a double row of lindens towers above the snow. These handsome shade trees produce an abundance of nectar, which in turn attracts swarms of bees that pollinate my flowers.

Naturalized daylilies (overleaf) provide a succession of bright flowers all summer long. They are surrounded by a large stand of white pines that I planted.

Among my first spring blooms are forsythia (opposite) and daffodils (above). In February, I cut a few branches of forsythia and put them in vases of warm water. When they bloom a few weeks later, it means that spring is right around the corner.

Daffodils, planted in fall, flower in March, soon followed by fragrant linden blossoms. Above, daffodils are shown in partial bloom around the base of a linden tree and, below, in *full* bloom.

The late Russell Page, a dear gardening friend, found these topiaries (right) for me many years ago. In summer, the topiaries need regular attention, while the lindens (left), in full leaf, require little care. When watering shrubs or any plant, there are a few basic rules to remember: Never water the day you spray; and water in the morning so that the leaves can dry before sundown—this keeps them free of mildew.

Make your garden cozy, blanket it, and protect it as if it were your child. Here roses have been covered with salt hay for the winter.

daughter of a Brahmin, she left Society for stage and films and, finding no satisfaction there, went adventuring in Mexico, where Diego Rivera painted her, aged twenty-two, as a honey-haired odalisque _desnuda_: a famous portrait that, according to legend, adorned a bar in Mexico City. Oh it must have been fun—but at heart she was too conservative, too _countrified_, for all that— she needed a home and a husband and dogs and horses and children (in that order) and flower gardens and vegetable gardens; and when she met the right man, the very massive but very gentle Winston F. C. Guest, she got them: houses, with gardens galore, in Old Westbury, Middleburg and Palm Beach.

Actually, when C.Z. first mentioned to me that she might be writing something, it didn't occur to me that the something would be about her horticultural concerns; I thought it would be about horses and dogs, for whom she has an animalistic affinity—indeed, I have never seen another human as at ease with dogs, as affectionate and yet in command, as Mrs. Guest. Soon, after we became friends, she invited me to visit her in Florida, and I remember watching her every morning hauling along the beach with nine or ten dogs at her heels—dogs who had nothing in common except single-hearted devotion to their blonde friend. _Honestly_, to use C.Z.'s favorite expletive ("Honestly, now I ask you, _honestly_"), you never saw such a confoundingly assorted gang —the purest-bred English Mastiffs, mutts from the pound, an Egyptian _Saluki_, a Golden

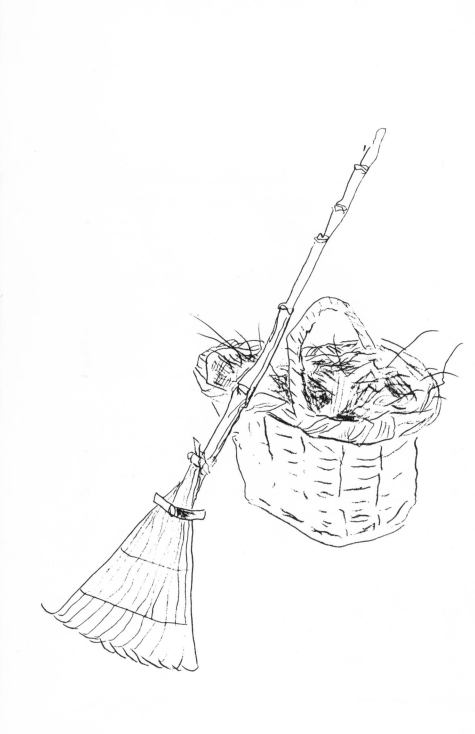

Labrador with a blind patch over one eye, a fat Peke huff-puffing to keep up, and, _everybody's_ particular buddy, including his fellow dogs, a big-sized Mexican Hairless that Winston had brought home after finding him abandoned in some Godforsaken Mexican airport; what made this dog so memorable, aside from his excitable Latin wit, was that he had only three legs: a hit-and-run driver had cost him one of the frontal two. Yet it made no difference—he was right there in full-flight, retrieving the driftwood C.Z. threw into the surf, and returning with it to be hugged: "Ah, good boy. Old soldier. My old soldier."

And it is enlightening, in a quiet way, and if you are lounging in the shade with a julep in your hand, to observe C.Z. exercising one of her horses. A decade or so past, _Time_ magazine published an extensive article on the upper-plateaus of American "aristocracy"—or however you choose to call it; and Mrs. Guest, as the magazine's top-selected exemplar, appeared on the cover in a very formal riding habit. Cold. Soignée. The Ice-Cream Lady. Maybe so. At horse shows. Or riding to hounds somewhere in Virginia. But usually, when observed galloping across the countryside, she is wearing cowboy chaps, and a man's shirt with rolled-up sleeves. She is certainly a finely-tuned sportswoman; and quite a sport, too.

A very _good_ sport—as I have every reason to know. Once, after many years of friendship had accumulated between us, we drove together from New York to California. It was a wild ride: on

LETTUCE

the road five days and nights in a car bursting
with the restless activities of two huge English
Bulldogs (mine), plus a big black cat named
Happy (also mine). Because of the animals, and
the reluctance of restaurant proprietors to entertain
them, we picnicked all the way, the dogs battling
with us over such roadside delicacies as Stuckey's
Chili-Dogs—chili-drowned hot dogs that we
washed down with quaffs of Chateau Lafitte
Rothschild quaffed straight from the bottle (Mr.
Guest having provided us with a hamper of festive
wines for our journey). No matter the emergency
—an escaped cat, a snow-storm in Arizona, an
encounter with a rude sheriff at a Georgia speed-
trap, running out of gas after dark on a Texas
highway—C.Z. could always cope, for she has the
kind of nature that is at its most graceful under
pressure.

A friend once asked me: "Do you know the
difference between the rich and—well, you and
me? Vegetables." "Vegetables?" "Vegetables! At
Babe Paley's table, or Bunny Mellon's or
Betsy Whitney's or Ceezie's—haven't you ever
noticed how extraordinary the vegetables are? The
smallest, most succulent peas, lettuce, the most
delicate baby corn, asparagus, limas the size of
cuticles, the tiny sweet radishes, everything so fresh,
almost unborn—that's what you can do when you
have an acre or so of greenhouses."

My friend's observation was true—a certain kind
of hostess always does serve exceptional vegetables,
though owning hot-houses is apparently not the
answer, for most of this elegant produce is grown

PARSLEY

21

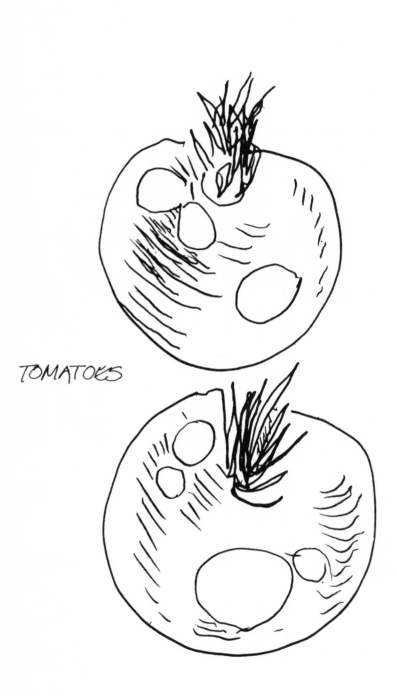

TOMATOES

in ordinary, if extensive, and extensively cared for, gardens. When I asked Mrs. Guest about this, she said: "The only thing I use hot-houses for is flowers and plants. Everything else is out of doors: raspberries, tomatoes, all that."

Templeton, the Guests' small and delightful estate in Old Westbury, has two hot-houses adjoining the rose-brick main house, and it is instructive to watch the mistress of the manor wandering around their misty, subtropical interiors adjusting a hyacinth here, straightening an orchid there: she seems so . . . exotic; and, I can't say why, a bit sinister like one of those ritzy enigmatic ladies in a stylish thriller. Perhaps the atmosphere of hot-houses, the quivering green light, the verdant haze scarcely rippled by slowly turning fans, makes everyone look like that.

But, once she has stepped across the threshold that leads from the glass houses to the walled garden that contains her row upon row of edibles and lookables, the true CeeZee emerges, like a sun sliding from behind the clouds. There, with her baskets and spades and clippers, and wearing her funny boyish shoes, and with the sun-borne sweat soaking her eyes, she is a part of the sky and the earth, possibly a not too significant part, but a part. And that is what this little testimony of Mrs. Guest's is about; well, yes, it is about gardening—but it's also about belonging, being a part of living things: just, you might say, life itself.

Truman Capote September 15, 1975

Foreword

So many friends have been asking me questions about their gardens that I have finally decided to do something about it. I am constantly receiving phone calls from people who have seen my garden and wonder how, with my busy schedule, I am able to keep my many, many plants, flowers, and vegetables in such fine shape. I simply tell them that I have a system, and now I would like everyone to know the C.Z. system so that they may discover the beauty and pleasure of raising and tending a garden. The C.Z. system is a pattern of rules to follow which will make gardening not only easy but lots of fun. Whether you follow my rules or make your own, the important thing is that you develop a pattern. This is the C.Z. system. This book isn't intended for any one group of people. It is for all who want to learn the ABCs of gardening and have fun doing it. The purpose of this book is to show what simple gardening has meant to me. I hope that through gardening you, too, will feel the inspiration I have felt.

One important word that every home gardener should remember is "simplify." If your garden is overpopulated with too many kinds of flowers, it may become a huge chore instead of a delight. At my house I have two gardens, a small "formal garden" around the terrace consisting only of roses, and what is known as a "kitchen garden" of flowers and vegetables. Of course there are many plants and flowers I would like to have but don't

A beautiful garden will give you an enormous sense of pride and accomplishment. Since I combine many different cut flowers in my house, I grow a great variety in my gardens. A favorite orchid, *Terete vanda*, grows best in full sunlight—the hotter the better!

Annuals are dependable, because you can be sure that they will bloom throughout the summer. Gloriosa Daisy (opposite) is an annual developed from the wild Black-eyed Susan; these tetraploid beauties are very easy to grow, and bloom profusely on long, sturdy stems.

'Fire Beacon' Swiss Giant Pansy (top), a dazzling annual, has huge flowers, up to 4 inches across. Grown from cuttings, these impatiens (bottom) are also annuals. Here they are a cheerful border along a brick wall.

'Fluffy Ruffles' Petunia (above), a showy, versatile annual, is grown in pots, beds, and window boxes. This hybrid bears enormous flowers, $5\frac{1}{2}$ to $6\frac{1}{4}$ inches across, displaying attractive veins and ruffles.

'Lady Betty Balfour' Clematis (right) is a lovely vine that provides beauty where no other plant can, and camouflages unsightly fences and walls.

Lantana (overleaf), a handsome shrub, is often a happy hunting ground for whiteflies and red spider mites!

Perennials, which, if properly cared for, will bloom for years without replanting, include these bearded irises (below). Irises add stately elegance to a garden in spring and are easy to grow in places with good drainage and full or afternoon sun.

Siberian Iris (right) blooms in early summer. It is easy to care for and exceptionally graceful.

Hyacinths (first overleaf) are among the loveliest of spring flowers—and irresistible to sniff. Here, large Dutch and little grape hyacinths, with their delicate spires of blue, make charming companions, appearing year after year.

While some geraniums are perennials, Martha Washington 'Can Can' geraniums (second overleaf) are woody like azaleas and are a favorite for window boxes, containers, or beds in the garden.

Hardy lilies are excellent in perennial borders, attractive among shrubs, and superb as cutting flowers. They are a cinch to grow in any good, well-drained garden soil. Here are three favorites: opposite, the gorgeous pink 'Gypsy', an Asiatic Hybrid Lily; top right, 'Pink Perfection'; and bottom left, 'Enchantment' lilies.

'May Sadler' Oriental Poppy (top left) is very showy, producing many huge, brilliantly colored blooms during May and June, year after year.
Graceful, airy flowers, columbines (bottom right) bloom from spring to early summer. They are charming favorites in the perennial border.

While some perennials, such as lilies, bloom from June to September, others, like these peonies, enliven my garden in late May or early June. A peony bud (top), alas, is still too young to reveal the feather-duster opulence of its fabulous open bloom.

The fragrant flowers of white peonies (opposite) can be 6 or 8 inches in diameter or more.

Since peonies and lilies grow quite tall, and a sudden June storm could ruin your garden, it is important to use tall, sturdy stakes for these flowers. This clump of peonies (bottom) is encircled by a wire-ring stake.

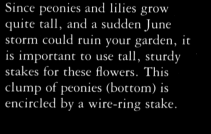

Japanese peonies (overleaf) have blossoms that are singles, having one or two rows of petals with bright yellow centers; other peonies may be doubles, having showy clusters of petals.

These chrysanthemums flower from August through October. They are a traditional autumn favorite in the perennial garden —beautiful, versatile, and long-lasting as cut flowers or as houseplants.

because it would require too much maintenance. Even with help I have to oversee everything that is done since young gardeners often mistake certain flowers and vegetables for weeds. I must confess, though, when I first started gardening, I pulled up a few vegetables myself, thinking they were weeds. I chuckle at the thought now every time I show a new gardener the difference. Don't think I haven't made mistakes!

There are so many fabulous things about gardening, and the best is that absolutely anyone can do it. It's great fun, and for someone who is unhappy or lonely, having a garden is like having a good and loyal friend. Gardening can also be a tremendous relaxation for someone who is nervous. I find that being outside and using my hands to care for each flower is very soothing. In addition, once you plant your garden you'll feel such a thrill to see your things growing. Each day you'll find it's different—a new surprise! After a good rain all the young flowers and vegetables seem to sprout right out of the earth, as if to say, "Here I am!" Your garden will help you discover a whole new world. Nature can never be hurried . . . her seasons come and go—they wait for no one. There is no way you can plant a row of green beans and have them ready to eat in three weeks. You must have a certain amount of discipline to keep your garden. If you do not take some care of it, you will find you are competing with the pests, bunnies, birds, and chipmunks. It will be a race to see who will get there first! You will also develop, as I have, a tremendous respect

for nature. She can never be bullied or made to
change her ways—she is truly Mother Earth.
For those consumed by the pursuit and exercise of
power, plant a garden—you will find one can't
impress Mother Nature.
Everyone today seems to be interested in "getting
back to nature." I think it's wonderful, especially
for young people. We are all becoming more and
more conscious of giving back to the earth what we
have taken out. Gardening will make you
appreciate something that many people have grown
to ignore—that we are all part of the mystery of
the earth's cycle of life. No scientist in the world
can make winter follow spring. It's rather a relief,
don't you think? Not even politicians can tamper
with the seasons! Think of what a mess they would
make if they could. We wouldn't know when to
plant our gardens. What confusion!
A beautiful garden will give you an enormous
sense of pride and accomplishment. It's great fun
deciding what colors you like best and then letting
your imagination run wild. I personally like
orange or yellow flowers the best, and I mix all
my different plants, flowers, and orchids together
in my house so they never get monotonous or
formal. You can get so absorbed in your
gardening, and there is always something to do.
You must keep up with it and tend to it every
day. It's like watching your children grow. It
will give back to you all the love and care you put
into it. Your garden is a good friend—a true
friend. And if you help it grow, it will never
disappoint you.

46

ROSE

VARIEGATED
PARROT TULIPS

Flowers

The other day a friend of mine called to tell me the latest news. She was in Miami Beach at a lunch party for visiting royalty, and as she strolled around the property, she thought it odd that she didn't see or hear one bird. She couldn't believe it . . . can you? It is hard to imagine a garden without birds. How sad it would be if everyone had fake lawns and flowers, don't you think? Let's start your garden now so that this doesn't happen to you.

Your First Garden

Wherever you are, be sure that the frost is out of the ground and the soil has begun to warm up before you start. First, you must get the proper tools. I suggest a rake, hoe, shovel, garden fork, and a lightweight hose for watering. Now you must decide what size you want your garden to be. I will use the example of twelve feet by twelve feet, which I think is a good size for a beginning garden. You may go smaller, but I suggest you do not go any larger, at least for the first year, until you gain some knowledge and confidence. Decide where you want your garden and then section off that spot by taking two stakes tied together by a piece of string twelve feet long. Put the stakes in the ground, stretching the string tight. Dig a little trench under the string in a straight line. This is the first side of your bed. Make sure it is straight, or you will have a zigzag bed! Now square off your garden by doing the same thing for the remaining three sides.

You have your bed—now you can get down to business. Take your garden fork and dig. Loosen up and turn over all the dirt until it is nice and light with no grass in it. Once you've loosened the earth, get some peat moss and some dry cow or sheep manure. Mix a little of each into the soil—enough to make it porous. This fertilizer must be worked through the soil completely so that it is thoroughly mixed into the dirt. Then rake your bed to smooth it out, making sure all stones and rocks are removed. Before you plant, the soil must be thoroughly moistened a good foot down, then let dry slightly until it is workable.

Now for your first row. Take your stakes and string and make a straight line from one end of the bed to the other, a few inches from the side, and make a two-inch trench down that line. This is your first row. Take your little package of seeds and sow them along the row that you have just made. Do not bunch the seeds, so that you will have enough for two rows. Then, with your hands, lightly cover the seeds with the soil. I suggest making two rows of each flower, whichever ones you like best. You may now go onto your next row. Each row should be about twelve inches apart. Plant each row of flowers the same way. Then give your garden a watering, but very gently, so as not to wash the seeds away. Some easy-to-grow flowers that I think you'll enjoy are zinnias, marigolds, gloriosa daisies, cosmos, sweet alyssums, sunflowers (which the birds love), and snapdragons.

A Strawberry Border

To make your garden pretty, I suggest putting strawberry plants around the border. You can buy them at your local garden center, and you won't have to buy too many because strawberry plants multiply. I think eight plants will do—one in each corner and one in the middle of each row. The strawberry plants send out runners with a little plant at the end of each. In the fall you can dig up these little plants and transplant them next to their parents.

Annuals

I would like to explain to you now the difference between annual and perennial flowers. The flowers I have suggested to you above are annuals, which means they must be replanted each year. These flowers are the most dependable because you can be sure that they'll bloom and give your garden color all summer long. When the flowers are finished, they can just be pulled out of the ground.

A thrifty trick that I use every year is this: I put yellow ribbons around the stems of the particular zinnias, marigolds, and daisies I like best. In the center of each flower there are many seeds. I let the flowers dry up on their stems, then cut off the wilted tops of the ones I have marked. I take these dried flowers, and store them on cardboard until completely dried. After a month or so I put the seeds in a bag, which keeps them dry until spring planting. As a result I never buy zinnia, marigold, or daisy seeds.

Perennials

The other flowers, called perennials, are flowers that if properly cared for can bloom for years without replanting. Some perennial flowers that I have in my garden are irises, peonies, lilies, primroses, day lilies, Oriental poppies, and sweet williams. Peonies and irises bloom in late May or early June, whereas the lilies and day lilies do not bloom until July, August, and September. Some other nice perennials that you might prefer are lupines, chrysanthemums, phlox, columbines, and delphiniums. Hollyhocks are really almost like a perennial because they reseed themselves, so I am including them in this list. Perennials can be planted in the spring, but I think that fall planting is preferable. They must be placed in a two-inch-deep hole with some peat moss or a mixed organic soil in the bottom and then covered with the dirt. The soil should be kept moist at all times.

One convenient thing about a perennial is that when the flower is finished for the season, you can just cut it down to the ground and forget about it until next year. With both annual and perennial flowers the best time to pick is in the early morning. Always pick your flowers when they are in bud (which means before they are fully opened). When picked at this time, the flowers will last longer and be more fragrant. Fresh-cut flowers absorb a lot of water, so put them in a deep vase and keep a close check on the water for the first day. Also, pull off all the lower leaves so that only the stem of the flower is in water.

AURATUM
LILY

51

Roses

I haven't mentioned roses, but I do think that everyone loves a rose. They take much more care than other flowers, so I suggest you start with just two or three bushes. Rosebushes are so easy to find nowadays. I see that they're sold in supermarkets and hardware stores, as well as in garden centers. You will find that roses are for sale continually from early spring until fall, but by far the best time to plant is in the spring. I suggest you buy container-grown roses; they are slightly more expensive, but they are the easiest to plant and will bloom the soonest. Just be sure to read the directions on the package. The diagrams on pages 62 and 63 are very easy for you to follow.

Cultivating Tips

Good drainage is essential in growing fine roses. Roses consume a lot of water but should not be planted where a standing pool of water can accumulate. This will kill any plant. Fertilize your roses in the spring with a little bone meal and once again in the middle of June. Then get some mulch, which can consist of many things, among which are cow manure, wood chips, leaves and pine needles, and spread it underneath the bushes at least two inches thick to keep the ground moist. When the mulch rots down, it adds to the soil an organic matter called humus, which is vital for good growth. In the spring cultivate this mulch into the soil to guarantee an increase in the humus content.

What a thrill you'll get picking your first rose. They are so beautiful, especially the long-stemmed hybrid teas, shown on these pages, the most popular group of roses. As they require more care than other flowers, I suggest starting with just two or three bushes.
Garden Party, a fragrant hybrid tea, blooms well in mid-season.

As a group, hybrid teas are varied, hardy, and produce flowers throughout the season. Peace (top) is the most well known hybrid tea, having won five first-prize medals for excellence. This climbing form often blooms sparsely for a few years until it establishes itself.

Granada (opposite), a prolific bloomer, has a spicy fragrance. It is resistant to disease, but needs protection from mildew and from severe winter conditions.

Known for its fruity fragrance, Medallion (bottom) was an All-American Rose Selection in 1973. This hybrid tea is most successful in an area with mild, cool weather.

Related to Peace (overleaf), this sport, or mutation, called Chicago Peace, has all the favorable characteristics of its parent, but is distinguished from it by its color.

Typically the flowers of hybrid teas have a spiral shape, with the petals unfurling evenly. Pink Peace (opposite) exemplifies this classic form. It blooms well in all seasons and is winter hardy, disease resistant, and very fragrant.

Perfume Delight (above), an All-American Rose Selection in 1974, has cup-shaped flowers with about half as many petals as Pink Peace. Blooming singly and in clusters, it produces an abundance of flowers in mid-season.

Double Delight, a prize-winning hybrid tea, is a special pleasure to watch as its classic blossom unfolds, revealing the varied combinations of its "double" color.

Importance of Pruning

Your roses must be pruned in the spring because they tend to lose their vigor after two, three, or four years and need to be replaced with young growth. Pruning concentrates growth on a select number of new shoots which are capable of producing first-rate blooms. The more severely a branch is cut back, the more vigorous will be the new growth sprouting from it. Cut the stronger shoots back eight to ten inches from the ground; all the weak and thin wood should be removed entirely.

Spring Cleaning

Always begin in the spring with a clean garden. As soon as the bushes have been pruned, drench the canes, the bud unions, and the immediate soil area with a spray of fungicide-insecticide to kill overwintering spores and insects. Phalton, isotox, or benlate mixtures seem more effective than dormant spray and are less likely to burn. Spray immediately. Repeat in a week. After pruning them, just make sure that your roses get plenty of sun and water during the dry months, and spray once a week. Always spray in the early morning before the sun gets too hot, to avoid sunburn of wet leaves. I do it on Tuesday so that I don't forget. This is part of the C.Z. system.

My Weekly System

Remember, it is essential that you follow some kind of pattern in tending your garden. As I said, I spray my flowers and vegetables on

Take the rose plant out of its pot, making sure the roots are undisturbed. The pot may be broken or upended.

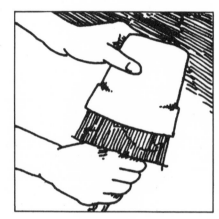

The hole for your rose plant should be the same size as for a bare root plant. Make the hole at least thirteen inches across. Mix peat moss in with the soil.

Make a mound out of the peat-soil mixture. Place the rose plant on top of it, again making sure the roots are undisturbed.

Fill up the hole carefully and water when done. Pack the soil down.

Tuesdays; I water them on Mondays, Wednesdays, and Fridays. Never spray your garden on the days that you water because the wet leaves will keep the spray from being effective. On the days that you water, do it in the morning so that your garden can dry off sufficiently before nightfall. If your plants are wet for a long while, they are susceptible to mildew, and roses especially are extremely prone to black spot as well as mildew. Shrub and old-fashioned roses, however, are quite hardy and resistant to diseases and bugs.

What a thrill you'll get picking your first rose. They are so beautiful.

How to Cut Roses

When you cut your roses, you must do it properly to keep the plant strong and healthy. The main shoots are covered with thorns, and small leaf-covered stems. The number of leaves on the stem varies, depending on where the stem is located on the shoot. In other words, the stems near the top of the shoot have only three leaves while stems near the middle of the shoot have five leaves and the lower stems can have seven or more. Always snip the main shoot at an angle just above the stems which have five leaves. If you pick your roses this way, you will find that new shoots will sprout from where you have cut, and your rose blooms will increase.

Don't forget—you can never give your roses too much care. You will be rewarded for all your work.

There is no need to mound the earth around plants that have started growing in pots; this would retard their growth. Check for weak canes, removing them with a hand pruner.

Wait a day or two, then spray your plant with an insecticide. If not yet in bloom, it will soon start producing flowers.

ROSE

Pruning Roses

The drawings at right show you the correct way to prune three different kinds of roses. There are many different approaches to correct pruning, but one thing to keep in mind is this: Besides the major pruning, which happens only once a year, prune a little bit all year round. Spent flowers need to be removed, and branches that tangle and cross should be trimmed back.

Pruning Fruit Trees

As for fruit trees, cherry, apple, and pear trees need only light pruning of damaged or inferior twigs and branches. But nectarines and peaches are just the opposite. If not pruned regularly, they can easily get out of hand. Remember that last summer's new growth will produce this year's fruit and flowers. So always leave some of the previous year's new growth, else your tree will not produce fruit.

Like peaches, apricots and plums grow quickly. But like apples, their fruit is produced on slow-growing short spurs. New branches that are too straggly or long can be removed completely without the loss of the entire fruit crop. Try, though, to leave at least a piece of each new branch.

Shaping Fruit Trees

Fruit trees are ideal candidates for the art of espaliering, that is, training plants to grow in specific shapes. Information and diagrams about this method of pruning are on pages 82 and 83.

Cut spurs along canes of climbers so two or three good buds remain. Prune standard rose to keep top open and symmetrical and to remove twigs.

From January (in mild climates) to early spring (in cold climates) you can prune dormant rosebushes. Remove weak stems, branches that cross, and the oldest canes.

Where the winter climates are mild, cut the canes back, leaving two-thirds of the plant. Harsher climates call for a half to two-thirds to be removed.

Old canes should be cut flush with the bud union. Stubs will rot and can damage the entire plant.

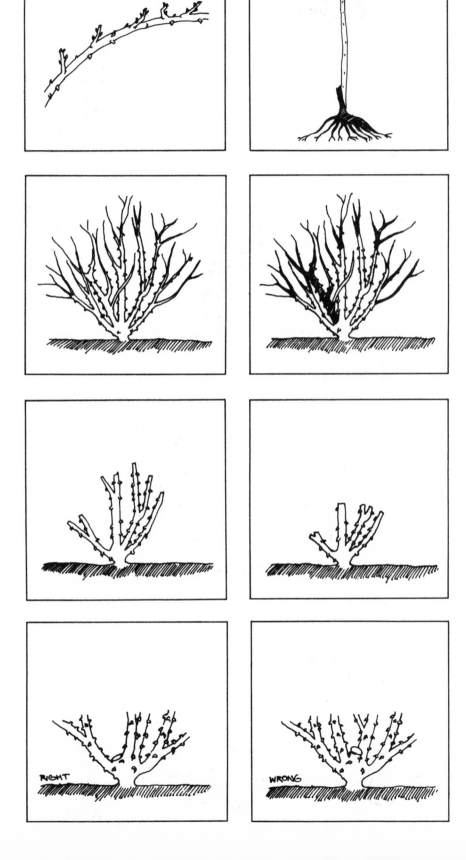

A soil and straw blanket

A cylinder of wire mesh

Styrofoam rose cones

The "Minnesota tip"

Winter Protection Methods

In preparation for winter, you should make your garden cozy by blanketing it and protecting it as if it were your child.

The first pair of diagrams at left (from top to bottom) show how to enclose a rosebush with a covering of soil and straw. Make a mound of soil about twelve inches high over the bud union of each bush (the soil should come from another part of the garden). After the mounds freeze, cover them with straw to keep them frozen.

In the second drawing soil is held in place around canes by a cylinder of wire mesh, which easily lets water drain away.

To use Styrofoam rose cones, canes must be tied together and cut down to fit the cones. A brick placed on top and soil over the flanges will hold the cone in place.

Another method is the so-called "Minnesota tip," which is used for bush roses. As illustrated, you dig up the roots on one side of the bush, bend the bush over into a trench, and cover it with soil.

At top right large bushes are protected by a cold frame with a hinged roof allowing for ventilation on warm days. Bend plant over bud union for "tipping" standards.

Climbers at bottom right should be protected with a soil mound in areas where winter temperatures range from 5 to 15 degrees.

Canes should be covered with soil if temperature drops below −10. For −10 to +5 degree weather, blanket plant with straw wrapped in burlap.

Cold frame

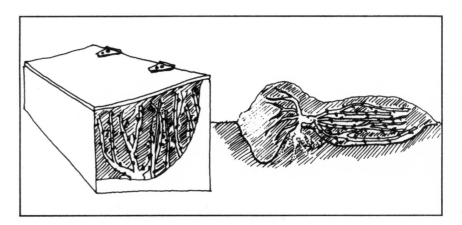

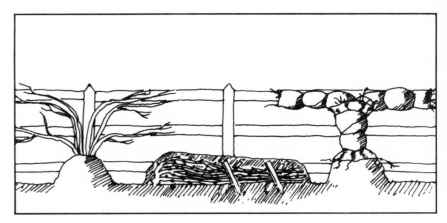
Straw wrapped in burlap

Importing Rosebushes

I would like to tell something interesting and useful that I found out several years ago when I imported some Duke of Windsor rosebushes from England. When brought in from other countries, flowers must go through the Agriculture Department for quarantine and inspection. There is an agricultural branch in every county. That was the first time I had ever had occasion to deal with men of the Agriculture Department, and I found them to be very nice, well educated, and helpful. These county agents came to my house three times that summer to check on the rosebushes. They told me that I was to keep any rosebushes that died so they could be burned, to ensure no spread of diseases. The men answered many questions and impressed me with their concern. I think that perhaps the Agriculture Department is the best-run branch of the government! Anyway, if you ever have any questions, I'm sure you will find the Agriculture Department to be most helpful.

One last tip. If you ever want to import various plants or orchids, you can apply to the Agriculture Department and they will issue you a number. This number is your identification and makes importing plants easier and faster for you.

At first, you will start out with a little knowledge and as you become absorbed with your rose garden, you will find your know-how increasing. And one day you'll wake up to discover you know quite a lot about gardening.

The kitchen garden, consisting of my favorite vegetables, is really my pride and joy. I can spend hours there digging, planting, picking, snipping, looking, inspecting, nibbling, and just plain relaxing!

All garden tools are kept in the garden house—and put away clean! Here dendrobiums, part of my orchid collection, hang on the garden house, their favorite vacation spot during summer.

Bibb lettuce and 'Red Sails' lettuce (opposite) are an attractive and tasty twosome. Keep lettuce seedlings on hand to fill vacancies in the garden as they occur. In summer, I plant heat-resistant types, but in September, I set out the same cool-weather varieties that I planted in spring, such as 'Ruby' Bibb and Buttercrunch.

Another pair of delicious and out-of-the-ordinary companions in your garden and in your salad are nasturtiums (overleaf) and 'Green Ice' lettuce.

Experienced gardeners have found that certain planting combinations actually enhance growth and reduce insect troubles. Baby carrots (above) are planted with compatible "bedmates," sugar snap peas.

Vegetables that may be eaten without cooking are an important part of my kitchen garden. One of the easiest vegetables to grow, rhubarb chard (opposite), does well in almost any type of soil. Its tender leaves can be added to salads.

A member of the cabbage family, purple kohlrabi (above) can be served like celery or carrots with a dip. One packet of seeds will yield a 20-pound crop.

Chives are a perennial part of my herb bed, which also includes mint, tarragon, basil, parsley, dill, rosemary, and thyme.

Vegetables and Fruit Trees

If you want to eat well this summer, you must plant your vegetables. Again I'll use a twelve-foot by twelve-foot bed as an example. You start your vegetable bed the same as you do your flower bed by sectioning it off with your stakes and string. Also use the same method to plant your vegetables as you did to plant your flowers. Again, I think it makes a vegetable garden very attractive to plant strawberries around the outside. You might also try some Bibb lettuce or parsley as a border to your garden. Some delicious vegetables for your garden are carrots, lettuce, beets, string beans, cabbage, corn, onions, and tomatoes.

There are many other vegetables which you may prefer, but the ones I have listed are the simplest ones for your first garden. Tomatoes may seem a little more difficult, but they are really quite easy to grow.

Raising Tomatoes

There are just a few essential differences in raising tomatoes and I will explain them to you now. All of the vegetables I have mentioned can be easily started from seeds with the exception of the tomato. Tomatoes can start from seeds, but really the easiest and best way to start them for your first garden is from small plants purchased at your garden center. Four or five plants are enough to take care of the average family for the summer. Tomatoes should be staked to grow well because if left on the ground, they will be eaten by various insects. You will need two-inch by two-inch stakes, six feet long, of cedar or redwood. Drive each stake about eighteen inches into the ground beside the plant. Plants should be twenty-four to thirty inches apart. When the plant is about fifteen inches high, tie it loosely to the stake. Each time the plant grows another fifteen inches, tie it again to the stake to keep the stem from sagging. When the plant reaches the top of the stake, you must pinch off the growing tip of the main stem for forced side branching.

Producing Delicious Vegetables

Spraying of your tomatoes and all your vegetables is easy because most of the new sprays contain insecticides and fungicides which will eliminate all the garden pests and diseases. Many of the sprays come in easy sprayer-top cans. Again, it is very important to read the directions on the can, as each spray may be different. Fertilization is also easy. Your vegetable garden should be done two or three times during the summer. It is best to fertilize lightly at frequent intervals rather than one heavy dose in the spring. Commercial fertilizers contain three important chemical elements: nitrogen, phosphorus, and potash, which will enrich your soil and produce good vegetables.

A few additional vegetables to try are squash, melons, zucchini, eggplant, and lima beans. For those of you who like cucumbers, I know of the latest thing—burpless cucumbers! (I don't have to explain that one, do I?) You can buy them at garden counters; just ask for burpless cucumbers!

ONION

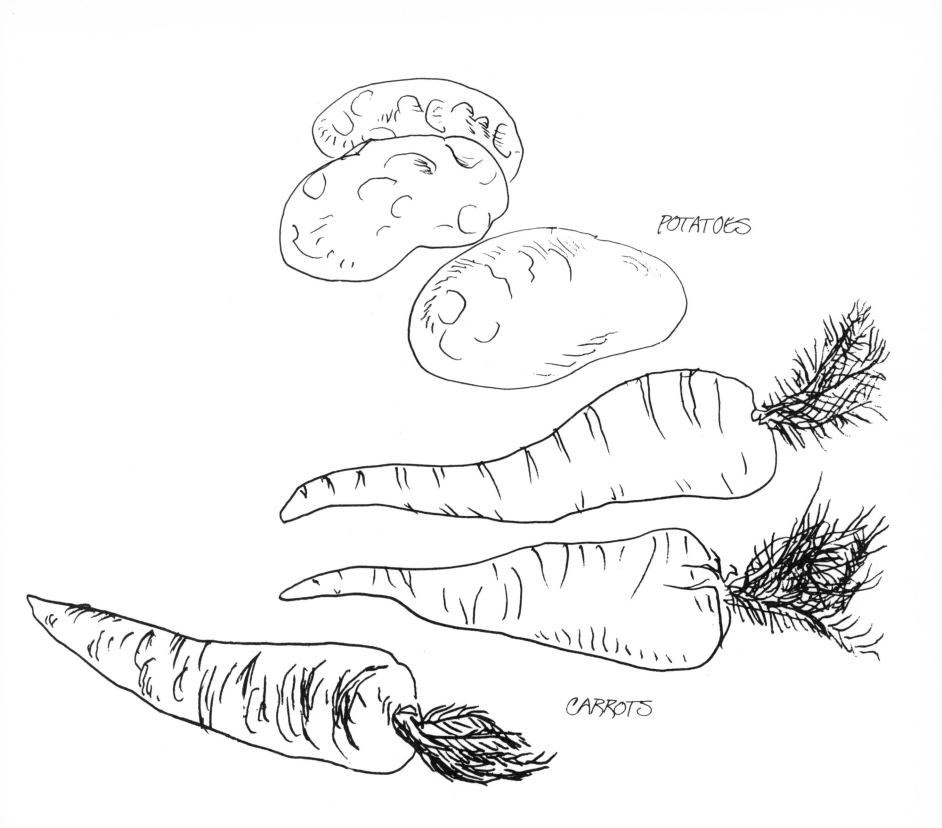

POTATOES

CARROTS

Early Spring
Plant as soon as the ground can be worked in spring: Broccoli plants • Cabbage plants • Endive • Kohlrabi • Lettuce • Onion sets • Parsley • Peas • Radishes • Spinach • Turnips

Mid-Spring
Plant these at time of the average last killing frost: Carrots • Cauliflower plants • Beets • Onion seeds • Parsnips • Swiss Chard. Plant two weeks later: Beans • Corn • Early potatoes • Tomato seeds

Early Summer
Plant when soil and weather are warm: Lima Beans • Cantaloupe • Celery plants • Crenshaw melons • Cucumbers • Eggplant plants • Pumpkins • Pepper plants • Potatoes for winter • Squash • Tomato plants • Watermelons

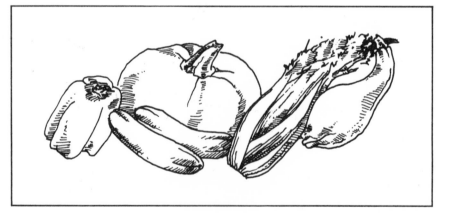

Mid-Summer to Fall
Plant in late June or early July: Beets • Broccoli • Cabbage • Cauliflower • Kohlrabi • Lettuce • Radishes • Spinach • Turnips

Planting in a Small Space

For those of you who are limited in space, such as people who live in apartments, it is very easy to grow beets, carrots, Bibb lettuce, and chard in twelve-inch redwood boxes. Just make sure the soil is moist and that there are holes in the bottom of the box for drainage. Other space savers are plants that grow vertically rather than horizontally. Use stakes and trellises for supporting vegetables such as tomatoes and cucumbers and string beans. You'll be surprised at the number of vegetables you can grow in a small space.

For those gardeners who are planting out of doors, the chart at left is a guide to growing seasons. This chart was prepared for Long Island residents, but it can be made to apply to any area where first frost occurs in October, and last frost in April. The harvest is extended by planting for fall and winter crops.

My Best Fruit Trees

Fruit trees provide yet another source of pleasure —plus, they are beautiful! I think it is great fun to grow your own peaches, pears, apricots, plums, and apples. I prefer the dwarf fruit trees because they are smaller but still produce the same amount of fruit as a larger tree. You can buy these dwarf trees from a nursery and plant them in the spring. Once you have planted your trees, don't get discouraged. It is generally advertised that fruit trees will bloom in two years, but I have found they do not bloom until three to five years.

STRAWBERRY PLANT

81

Dig a deep, wide hole, at least six inches wider and deeper than the tree's root ball. If you are planting a large tree, make the hole even wider and deeper to ensure the new roots easy penetration.

Put the topsoil in the bottom when refilling (after mixing it with peat or compost), to encourage root growth. Save the subsoil for filling the upper part of the hole.

Put the root ball in the hole at the same depth as it was in the nursery. Measure the root ball, fill up the bottom with the topsoil-peat mixture, and place the tree.

Do not put fertilizer in the bottom of the hole. Spread a ring of food around the top of the filled-in hole after planting. The plant food should be four inches from the trunk, and it should be scratched into the surface.

The diagrams below will be easy to follow. It is very important to spray your trees in the early spring before the buds start to come out. This kills any insect eggs which have collected on the tree during the winter. The spray is called a dormant spray, composed of lime and sulfur, and must be applied only on a mild day when the sun can dry it quickly.

Espaliering

You might like to have your fruit trees espaliered. I have them in my garden and find them very elegant. The prettiest gardens I have seen in Europe all have espaliered trees, and if you would like to try them, there are many nurseries that specialize in them. In case you don't know, espaliering is training a plant or small tree to grow into a definite pattern. Fruit trees are most often used because when espaliered, most of their branch surface is exposed to the sun and therefore stimulated to produce more fruit. Apples, peaches, pears, apricots, and plums are favorite espaliered trees and are a good choice to plant in your vegetable garden.

If your garden is in a warmer climate, give an eastern exposure to your trees so the fruit won't be burned by reflected heat. On the other hand, colder regions dictate choosing a southern site.

Make sure your supports are sturdy; when full of fruit, branches are heavy. Use posts of galvanized wood or pipe (four by four inches), and stretch fourteen-gauge galvanized wire tightly on turnbuckles. Remember to leave four to twelve

After you have filled the hole with two-thirds of the topsoil-peat mixture, water, but don't drown, your tree.

Build a shallow ring of soil some two inches high around the trunk about a foot out.

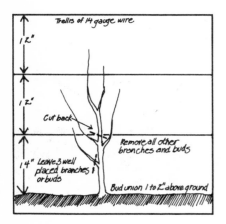

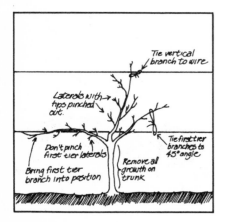

Planting time. Your newly planted tree is supported by a wire, strung north to south, with turnbuckles that can be tightened. Tie first-tier branches to wire; remove all others.

Growing season #1. Slowly train first-tier branches to grow horizontally. Tie the growing vertical branches to the next wire. Pick two young branches for next tier and pinch tips of any others.

inches between wall and trellis so air can circulate. Young dwarf fruit trees need very little pruning —only removal of branches that are too close together for the development of a well-balanced tree. As with all other trees, the best time to prune is in the early spring before the sap begins to run. If you happen to live in an apartment with a terrace or balcony in a city, why not try one or two espaliered trees in wooden tubs? They would be very impressive in a terraced garden and quite easy to care for as they are small.

There are many different ways to espalier trees; the diagrams here show you one of them.

Tips for Success

In caring for all your vegetables and fruit trees, remember to develop an easy-to-follow pattern. I systematically water every Monday, Wednesday, and Friday. If it is extremely hot and dry, however, and your vegetables begin to look a little "limpy," by all means water some more! Remembering: Never, but never spray the day you water! Mulch your vegetables as you do your flowers to keep the ground moist and also to keep the weeds down. This will save you a lot of work —weeding is such a bore.

One last point I want to make is to be sure to put a small mesh wire fence around your vegetable garden. You are not the only one who is hungry! You can imagine the disappointment you would feel after working hard to plant and care for your garden and then find that it has been eaten by someone else!

Growing season #2. The second-tier branches should be trained in the same manner as the first tier. All laterals below the second tier will produce fruiting spurs at their base, and fruit will appear in a year.

Dormant Season #1. Head the vertical branch back below the second wire as soon as the tree loses its leaves. Two branches should be left for the second tier, any others cut back to stubs with two or three spurs.

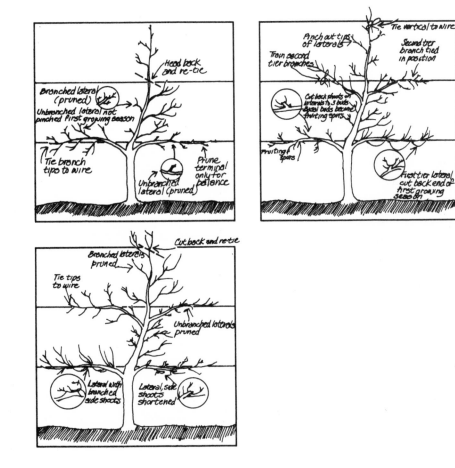

Dormant season #2. Head the vertical branch back below the third wire. Second-tier laterals should be pruned as were the first tier. Continue to train, keeping tree to designated shape.

So now that everything is planted and cared for, just sit back, relax, and wait for your garden to grow!

Bulbs

For those of you who want to prepare your own soil and plant your bulbs from scratch in pots, I find it best to mix together equal amounts of potting soil, topsoil, peat moss, and perlite. This mixture has sufficient nutrients for plant growth and development and should be easy to work and easy for the plant roots to penetrate. All bulbs are planted in the fall and will bloom the following spring, whether they are started in pots or planted outside in the ground. Daffodils, tulips, hyacinths, crocuses, freesia, and narcissus should be potted in eight- to ten-inch pots. In the bottom of each pot put pieces of broken clay pots or stones for drainage, and then fill the pot with this mixed soil a little above half. Put in six to eight bulbs so that they almost touch one another—be sure the pointed tips are up—then cover the bulbs with soil until the tips are just slightly under the surface. Leave an inch below the rim of the pot, then water your plant thoroughly. Now that the bulbs are planted, place the pots outside and cover them with two inches of sand. Leave them outside for the winter because the cold air will stimulate the roots to grow.

If you have rodents around your house, you should protect the bulbs by putting a covering of mesh wire over each pot.

ANEMONE
TULIP
POLYANTHUS

RED DOUBLE
TULIP

Spring Flowering

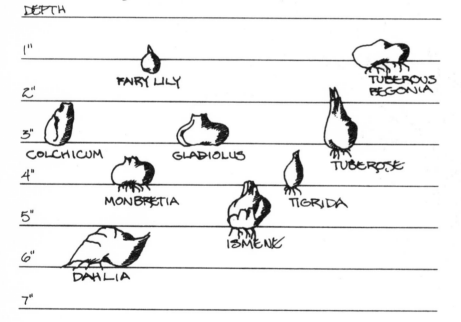

DEPTH

1"

2"

3" CHIONODOXA CROCUS GRAPE HYACINTH SCILLA SNOWDROPS

4"

5" HYACINTH

6" DAFFODIL LILY TULIP

7"

Summer Flowering

DEPTH

1" FAIRY LILY TUBEROUS BEGONIA

2"

3" COLCHICUM GLADIOLUS TUBEROSE

4" MONBRETIA TIGRIDA

5"

6" DAHLIA ISMENE

7"

Planting Holes

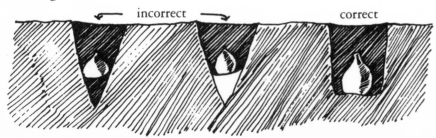

incorrect   correct

88

In the spring, when your little plants stick their heads out of the sand about two inches, it is time to bring them in. Shake or lightly brush off all the sand.

The newly exposed plant is very delicate and can't stand a lot of sun right away, so it is best to put all the plants off in a corner and cover them with newspaper for about two weeks. During this time they should be watered slightly twice a week. After two weeks you can take the newspaper off and place your plants near a sunny window. Continue watering twice a week and just wait for all your beautiful flowers to bloom. If everything goes well, you'll have lovely flowers for Easter.

As I mentioned earlier, when your flowers are finished, you can replant them outside in your garden. Old bulbs or any new bulbs should be planted in the ground in the fall according to the chart at left.

Blooming Timetable

Bulbs do not all come up at the same time. Some bloom in very early spring, while others can bloom up to three months later. I've worked out a list which will give your garden blooming bulbs from March to June.

Earliest tulips are Fosteriana, Single Early, Greigii, and Greigii Hybrids. You'll find Temple of Beauty, Red Riding Hood, and Oriental Splendor in this early group—they're best suited for rock gardens, early cutting beds, borders, pots, and planters. They'll bloom soon after your super-early winter buttercups, crocuses, hyacinths, and daffodils.

Next come the mid-season tulips—Darwin Hybrid, Triumph, Mendel, and some Greigii Hybrids. For splashes of bright color, plant these two inches apart. They are most effective in beds of all one variety.

The beautiful late tulips—Darwin, Cottage Parrot, Lily-Flowered, and Fringed—reach their peak in May and are especially colorful for cutting.

Double Date, or Peony-Flowered tulips, linger longest of all—these double-flowered tulips have sturdy stems and are ideal for mass plantings, borders, as well as for cutting.

Potted Herbs

I think it is fun to have a few potted herbs in the kitchen. Keep them in a sunny window and you will have herbs for cooking all year round. If you want, in the summer you can always transplant your herbs outside into your vegetable garden. I like chives, basil, rosemary, mint, oregano, savory, and sage. All of these will grow beautifully in your kitchen window as long as they have several hours of sun each day. Again, don't overwater.

Fruit Trees

Also available in pots at some garden centers are miniature lime, lemon, and orange trees, which are particularly nice because of their lovely fragrances.

PANSY
FORGET-ME-NOT
PRIMROSES

Flats

There are certain advantages in starting your seeds indoors in flats. (I use discarded egg cartons.) It is the best method to use for expensive or fine seed or seeds that take a long time to germinate and grow (including most perennials). Flats can be good for some annuals and vegetables that you want to start while the ground outside is still too cold or wet. In flats you can control the soil mix and place the plants where they will get just the right amount of sunlight or shade. There is also very little danger of insects.

Getting Started

Flats are usually four inches high and should be filled with potting soil about halfway. Be sure there are holes in the bottom of the flat for drainage. With a pencil, mark off your rows in a straight line, pushing the pencil into the soil about one-half inch. The rows should be two inches apart. You may plant any seeds you like in any order, but I suggest planting one kind of seed per row and then using garden markers to label each row. Cover the seeds lightly and gently dampen the soil with a syringe so as not to wash them away. The soil should be kept damp. Then cover the surface of the flat with a pane of glass or a wet newspaper to keep the moisture in. Put the flats in a warm spot but not in direct sun. Try to control yourself—don't peek for four or five days! In about a week your little seeds should appear. When they've come up about one-half inch, remove the

DEEP PURPLE
PANSY

91

glass or newspaper and move them into an area of filtered sunlight, as they are still too tender to take full sun. In eight to ten weeks they will be ready to be transplanted wherever you want them.

In case you are not aware, there are many new, ingenious short cuts to this method. You can buy seed-starter kits that have compact nutrient-filled containers, with the seeds already planted. All you do is remove the lid of the container and water. Everything has been done for you. You can also buy what are known as Jiffy Pots. Seedlings started in them can be planted, pot and all, in the ground at the proper planting time. The roots will grow right through the soil-like walls of the pot. I really think that these new methods are the best— they make starting seeds extremely easy and I suggest that everyone try them. This is what I do.

Plants

Plants are generally kept in the house in pots. Flowering plants have become my favorites because they are so easy to care for and they are especially nice for apartment dwellers—nothing can cheer up an apartment better than a bright plant.

How to Water Plants

The _worst_ and most common bad habit you can have is to overwater your plant. For some reason people think that plants have to be swimming in water. Plants are not fish! They must have a day or two to dry out or they'll drown. Do as I do— water only three times a week. Of course, in the

The pride we feel when admiring a carefully nurtured plant is doubled when we remember that the plant was once a tiny seed or bulb in the palm of the hand.

Clivia plants, which are bulbs, come from South Africa. In spring they produce flowers in clusters, and the plant may reach a height of two feet.

Good care, periodic pruning,
and, if possible, some time
outdoors, will help to extend the
life-span of these garden
houseplants.

Some common houseplants can
be purchased as seeds from
catalogues, including geraniums
and begonias. Shown here are a
few favorites taking in some sun:
Scented Geranium (*Clorinda*) (top
row, left); *Jasminum nitidum*
(right); *Plectranthus coleoides*
(bottom row left); white wax
begonia (right); and red
geraniums (overleaf).

Most commonly found in
Florida, where it has naturalized,
Moses-in-the-Cradle (*Rhoeo*),
above, comes from Nicaragua. It
has 3-petaled white flowers in
clusters held by a "boat-shaped"
bract—hence the name.

Carnations, among them this dwarf fragrance carnation (top left), have spicy fragrant flowers, and are wonderful as houseplants and for cut flowers. Plant them in well-drained, sandy or loose soil in full sun.

I plan the greenhouse around my favorite holidays, Thanksgiving and Christmas. Every room in the house is overflowing with fragrant paper-white narcissus (top right).

It is difficult to find any houseplant that has as much to offer as the African Violet (opposite). Its foliage is attractive, and it produces flowers during most of the year. Streptocarpus (bottom left), also known as the Cape Primrose, is another wonderful houseplant. Related to the gloxinia and African Violet, it thrives under the same tender care as its cousins.

Amaryllis—white, red, and orange, gloxinias (bottom right), African Violets, and red poinsettias.

With daily watering and lots of sun, a poinsettia will last from the Christmas holiday season until April. The majestic head is a bronze goose from the Ming dynasty, a 25th anniversary present to my husband.

winter they need even less watering. I mean it. _Don't overwater_. I know a really neat timesaving trick for watering. Put two or three ice cubes in the pot, depending on how big the plant is, and the water will just seep in slowly. Do this instead of dousing the plant with water. There are only a few plants that can really stand a lot of water. Two that I know of are hydrangeas and chrysanthemums.

Easy Care Favorites

The amaryllis is one of my favorite plants. It needs almost no care, just a little water, and no matter what you do, it seems to flower. I also think geraniums are nice. If you feed a geranium twice a month with a little plant food it can last for years. Some other nice summer plants are petunias, begonias, agapanthus, gloxinias, and impatiens. There are also some nice late fall and winter plants, such as chrysanthemums. They come in many different colors, shapes, and sizes, even dwarf for those who like small flowers. Many lovely prepotted bulbs available at garden centers are especially prepared to bloom at Christmastime, such as narcissus, hyacinth, and crocus. These will last several weeks and require only a little watering. After your bulbs have finished blooming, do not cut the foliage, as it is food for the plant the following year. It is best to let them dry up completely in the pot. They can be planted in the ground in fall and will bloom the following year—or give them to a friend who lives in the country so that someone else can enjoy them.

Gro-Lamps

Another fairly recent development is the method of growing plants with a fluorescent light. It is just like owning a greenhouse—you can grow anything, any time of year, by merely turning the lights on or off. Thirteen to sixteen hours of light are sufficient for most plants to bloom, but some need as much as eighteen hours. You can really grow anything you like—bulbs, seedlings, begonias, orchids, or perennials. With Gro-Lamps you have complete control of soil, moisture, and light conditions. For prime growing conditions you should have a timer switch which turns the lights on and off automatically. This will make sure the plants get the right amount of light daily, even if you are away from home. On a Gro-Lamp stand with plastic trays you can put hundreds of little plants in a small place. It is really an enchanting way of having a garden right in your living room all year round.

A Lean-to

Of course, another great way to grow plants or nearly anything you want out of season is with your own greenhouse or lean-to. A lean-to is the most economical because it needs only three sides, the fourth side being your own house, which provides heat. Lean-tos are made of glass and are really just a small greenhouse. They should be erected on the sunniest side of your house. The best kind of lean-to is the one with aluminum frames that need no maintenance. They can easily be put

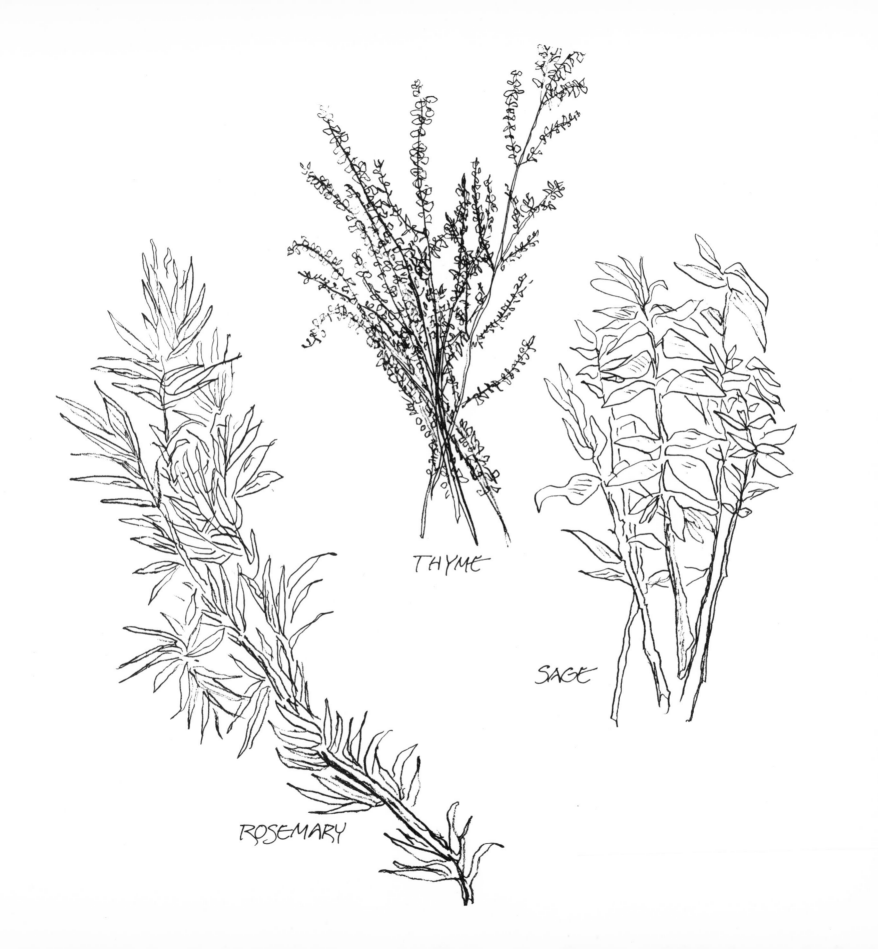

THYME

SAGE

ROSEMARY

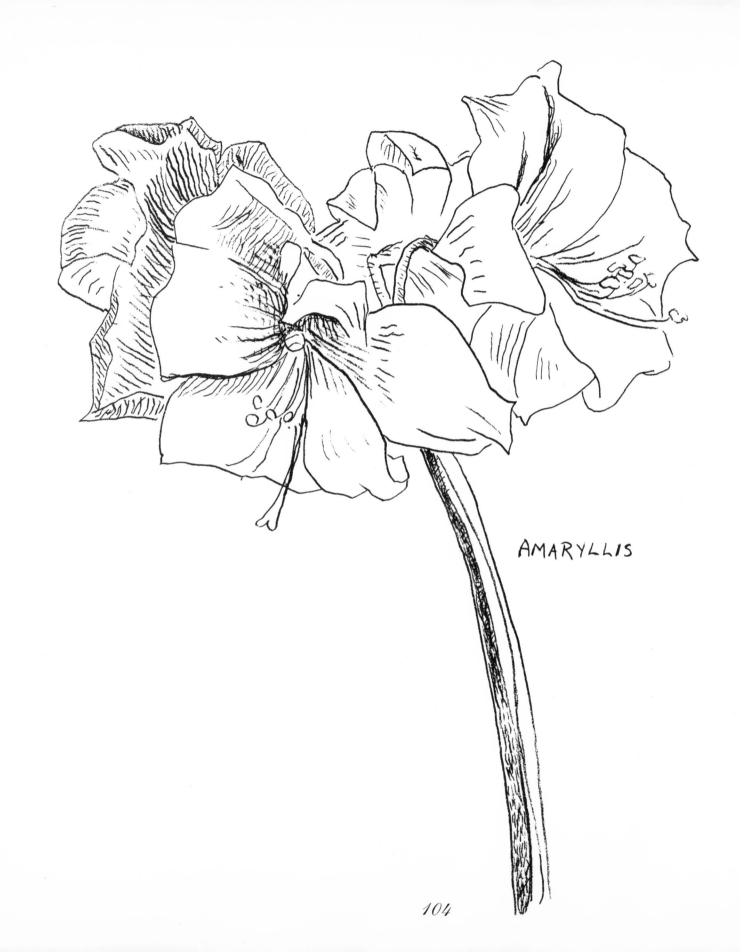

AMARYLLIS

up by a carpenter, or if you happen to be ambitious, you could probably do it yourself, since directions and diagrams are included with the lean-tos. They come in any size desired and can be ordered with a number of optional devices to make your indoor gardening quite easy and delightful, such as automatic ventilation systems, sprinkling systems, fans, and humidifiers.

Avoiding Plant Disease

An important thing to remember if you do have a greenhouse is _cleanliness_. Cleanliness is one of the greatest enemies to all plant diseases. Pests love rotting and decaying leaves, slime and slush, also rotting sawdust and shavings. I use fresh gravel for the greenhouse floor. If you have wooden benches, they should be made of redwood. When your plants are moved outside for the spring, nothing beats galvanized piping and galvanized steel mesh for clean, disease-free benches. Of course, you can have brick or concrete walks, but they are more expensive. That is why I suggest gravel.

Greenhouses

A greenhouse is almost the same as a lean-to but more expensive because it is a separate building and must be heated separately. I have two greenhouses, which are heated by oil. One greenhouse is just for orchids. It is in several sections, each section housing different species of orchids; for instance, one section is just for cymbidiums and another is for cattleyas. Luckily, most orchids can be grown together in the same climatic condition, and even if

POLYANTHUS

105

they're a little different, they will usually adapt themselves. My second greenhouse is also in sections. One area is just for my acid-loving plants, such as hydrangeas, hibiscus, azaleas, and camellias with another section for growing seeds, bulbs, and plants. I get so much enjoyment from my greenhouses—in fact, I practically live in them, especially in the late fall and winter and, naturally, around Christmastime. For one who loves plants as much as I do, it is the most delightful way to pass the day or, better yet, the year.

Lawns

I swore to myself that I would not mention lawns in my book, because there is nothing more exasperating in this world than trying to grow a beautiful lawn. Several people have asked me about lawns, however, so I will just say this: It's for the birds!

No matter what you do or how much you work or how much money you spend, you can never completely get rid of crabgrass—mainly because the birds carry the seeds on their wings and feet from one place to another. I've found it's an endless battle. I suggest that you just plant your lawn and do the best you can. There are so many books on lawns that I just don't want to discuss them. The more I try to kill my crabgrass, the more it grows. If you want to be happy with your lawn, do as I do. I just adore my crabgrass!

LILY OF
THE VALLEY

ANEMONE
HYACINTH
WHITE
DAFFODIL

107

Shrubs and Birds

No house or garden is complete without shrubs. There are shrubs for every climate, so everyone should have some. They can be of many different shapes and sizes—some are green and some are flowering. I like the flowering shrubs best.

Choice Azaleas and Lilacs

Around my house I have Exbury and Knaphill azaleas in brilliant colors of yellow and orange, and I have Azalea Schlippenbachii around the stable, which have beautiful rose-pink flower clusters, because my racing colors are red and old rose. I also have some lovely lilacs in my garden. There are two new and rare varieties of lilacs from Korea, and because of their origin, they are extremely hardy and will do well in all parts of this country. They are ideal for small gardens or small properties, as they never grow more than three feet high. They are called dwarf Korean lilacs, and the two varieties with which I am familiar are Miss Kim and Palibiniana. They are very unusual because they bloom later than other varieties of lilacs. Miss Kim is an ice blue and Palibiniana is a deep red. Both have a heavenly fragrance.

Other Special Shrubs

My favorite hydrangea is the Paniculata Grandiflora. Its flowers start out white and gradually change to a bronzy pink as the shrub ages. It is a Japanese variety and is extremely

APPLE
BLOSSOM

ORANGES

FORSYTHIA

hardy, as are the azaleas. The hydrangeas and azaleas both need an acid soil, plenty of humus, and a deep mulch all year round. They do well in full sun. One of my favorite shrubs is the Mock Orange, which has a divine fragrance—old-time gardeners sometimes call it Sweet Syringa. There are many varieties of Mock Orange, and one is as pretty as the others. Here are four. Enjoy a fragrant spring, summer, and fall with these varieties: Clethra Ainfolia Rosea, Enchantment (best double Mock Orange), Syringa Maude Notcutt lilac (white), and Syringa Daphne lilac (pale-pink flower). Another favorite is Hypericum Sungold, which has a lovely yellow flower but not much scent. Of course, I adore Hybrid Hibiscus with flowers of orange, red, or yellow, but unfortunately they are not hardy here on Long Island. In the summer I keep a few in pots around the terrace. Then in the fall they go back into the greenhouse. I do have some, though, at my house in Florida, planted around the tennis court. One of the first and loveliest shrubs to bloom in spring is the flowering quince. A pretty variety is called Pink Lady. It grows to only five or six feet, so it would be perfect for a small garden. Another shrub, not often seen, is the hardy Daphne Somerset. It is very easy to grow and has a wondrous fragrance. This shrub is quite hardy and needs little protection from the winter, but it does like a warm location in well-drained soil. There is a lovely Daphne Genkwa which flowers in various shades of blue. This variety is ideal for flower borders, rock gardens, or in front

WHITE
CAMELLIA

111

LILAC

of shrub borders, since it grows only three feet high. There are other varieties of shrubs which produce berries. The birds simply adore them! Please don't forget the birds. Pyracanthea-Firethorn is one of my favorites because its orange-scarlet berries stay on the bush well into the winter and provide food for the birds. Viburnum Opulus Xanthocarpum produces golden-yellow berries in immense clusters and also feeds the birds well into winter.

If you have a small shrub garden, you will naturally want to plant small shrubs. Here they are. Cydonia Knaphill, Forsythia Lynwood Gold, Spiraeas Snowbound, Hydrangea All-Summer Beauty, Hypericum Sungold, and Caryopteris Heavenly Blue will give your garden color all spring, summer, and fall, and each is only three to four feet high. All the shrubs I have named should be planted just like small trees, so consult your planting chart for directions. Shrubs are quite simple to care for, needing only to be fertilized in the spring and fall and kept well mulched.

Fall Flowering Shrubs
There are several shrubs that flower in the fall but are not often seen. One is Stewartia Pseudo-camellia, which has beautiful white fragrant flowers; because of the form of its blossoms, it is often referred to as imitation camellia. In the late fall the foliage turns to a red and golden yellow. Cornus Kousa Chinensis (Milky Way) is another fall bloomer and has large strawberrylike fruit and scarlet foliage.

ROSE
(ETOILE D'HOLLANDE)

Vines and Vinelike Shrubs

I do not want to forget to mention vines and vinelike climbing shrubs. They provide beauty where no other plant can. They are especially useful in camouflaging unsightly fences and buildings, and they require almost no ground, space, or care. You really do not see vines too much in America, but in England even the smallest cottage gardens have them winding up a wall or fence.

I have two beautiful vines in my garden which bloom throughout the summer. Each is a different variety of Bignonia— (Campsis) Trumpet Vine. One is Madame Gallon—the flowers are a rich apricot tinted orange with a fine dark-green foliage. The other is Yellow Trumpet with flowers of apricot yellow. They are both perfectly hardy and immune to all insects. They grow fast and need no support, as they fasten themselves easily to any fence or wall.

Another beautiful vine which does especially well on walls is the clematis, of which there are many different varieties. Mountain Rube is an early-blooming pink vine, whereas Clematis Paniculata is a late bloomer, flowering in August and September. My favorite is the Clematis Tangutica, which comes from China. It has masses of yellow flowers and it blooms all summer through fall. There are also some lovely hybrids available which are very different and fun to have. When planting your vines, the most important thing to remember is that the hole should be dug one foot away from the wall or fence—never any

CLEMATIS

closer. The hole for the clematis should be several inches larger and deeper than the size of the roots. This extra room provides a good root run for our vine, enabling it to grow well and produce many more flowers. Once the vine is planted, three-quarters of the top growth should be cut back and the remaining crown covered with two or three inches of earth. Then just add a light mulch to keep your vine moist. It will be the envy of all your neighbors!

Your Plants in Summer

One final thought . . . for those of you who go to the country during the summer, take your plants with you so that they can have a vacation, too. If you live in the country, put your plants outside for the summer. They love the fresh air and sunshine just as you do. An important thing to know is that the morning sun is the very best sun for your plants. The afternoon sun can burn the leaves, so if possible, shade your plants in the afternoon, especially during the hot, dry months of July and August. Then, in the fall when the nights get below sixty degrees, take your plants inside. Spray them first to get the bugs off. You will be amazed how much they have grown.

Attracting Birds

Since I've mentioned birds several times in this chapter, I feel that this is a good place to tell you how to make more little friends. Many people think that they need to put out bird feed only in the winter. This is not true. In the spring and

My interest in orchids was started by my mother. After I married, she sent me orchid plants each year for my birthday, Christmas, and my wedding anniversary.

Known as the "moth" orchid, *Phalaenopsis* (first overleaf) includes a number of exquisitely beautiful hybrids. They are ideal for a greenhouse, a sunny garden, or a humid sun room.

Other orchids in my collection include (second overleaf, left to right): yellow and green Cattleya, the best-known genus, because these flowers are often made into corsages; Orange Ascocendrum, a long-lasting dwarf orchid from Asia with bright, inch-wide flowers; and green and blue Zygopetalum, a fragrant species that grows to 40 inches tall and bears an extraordinary 4-inch blue and green flower—the rarest flower colors in the plant world.

Orchids are more rugged than most people think and can stand more abuse than many other plants. However, they have three requirements for optimum growth and bloom: the right temperature, the right amount of light, and adequate humidity. Cattleyas (below and opposite) are so hardy that they will flourish in your house or in a moderately warm (55°F to 60°F) greenhouse.

An explosion of beauty, multi-colored Cattleyas produce flowers in a wide range of colors from subtle pastels to dazzling shades. New colors are created each year.

Since there is an abundance of hybrid Cattleyas available, this popular genus includes something for every taste in color, size, and flowering season. Sometimes I like to try daring combinations of flowers at home, mixing potted orchids, such as this multi-colored Cattleya, with cut flowers to create wonderfully exotic arrangements.

summer there is very little natural food available to the birds. It is not until fall that the birds find the necessary wild seed in nature. If you want a wide range of birds in your garden, put out bird feed all year round. There are a variety of feeds available to attract a variety of birds. In addition to food, birds also appreciate water and birdbaths. After all, we all love to bathe! In the winter especially, birds suffer from a lack of water because everything is frozen. You can easily buy a little birdbath heater which will keep your birds happy and healthy, and the feed you put out will keep them warm in the frozen months of the year. (The feed keeps the birds fat, which insulates their bodies in the winter.) In my garden I have several different feed stations. I also have a wonderful window feeder, attached directly to the window, which enables me to see my little birds even when I am inside.

The Audubon Society

I have several bird houses around my garden. You know, birds have housing problems just as we do! To solve my birds' problems I rely on the Audubon Society. They have many attractive bird houses for various kinds of birds. There are big houses and small houses, because all birds _can't_ live together. Most birds have their own territories, but there are always a few big bullies lurking around. Little birds need their little houses to escape such a menace. The Audubon Society has just the right housing for the requirements of various species.

ORCHID

126

Orchids

I really have no set plan on how to arrange flowers. I love all different flowers together, and I find that almost all flowers and plants compliment one another. As I said before, I prefer orange and yellow flowers, but at Christmastime I love festive red and white ones. I also do something that very few people would ever dream of doing. I mix orchids with other flowers. They are really the most beautiful of all—each is unique and individual and they come in different shapes, colors, and forms. And some are almost too beautiful for words. I never tire of looking at one.

Growing Orchids

They are usually quite easy to grow, but orchids can sometimes be like people—some need to be pampered more than others. You probably have the idea that orchids are quite expensive; it's not true! I know a commercial-orchid grower in Florida who has a fantastic idea. His greenhouse is like a supermarket. Inside the door are three large tables just packed with multicolored, multishaped orchids, each table having a different price range. You can study and compare all of these beautiful orchids and then choose the one or ones you like best, ranging in price from only $5 up to almost $25. Fortunately, or unfortunately for me, I pass by this marvelous place each day on my way back from riding my horses. I almost always have an irresistible urge to stop in . . . just to look around, of course. I really cannot help myself—I buy one or two. So you see, by the end of the season I have quite a collection. Once you get interested, you will find that the hobby of collecting orchids is a never-ending quest. A few of the species I like are paphiopedilums, cymbidiums (also miniature), epidendrums, dendrobiums, calanthes, miltonias, oncidiums, renantheras, zygopealtum, vandas, and cattleyas. Everyone can afford to buy an orchid plant, and I think that everyone should. Just for fun, go out and buy one and see what happens. It can be quite a challenge to get your orchids to bloom every year, and when you become a really good gardener, you may even be surprised and get them to bloom twice a year. In every big city there is an orchid society, and if you call, I'm sure they will be only too happy to give you advice on caring for your orchid. You may make some new acquaintances. I have. Who knows, you could become a hobbyist just like me!

The Way I Use Flowers

Getting back to flower arrangements, I love to use lilies. The colors and varieties are incredibly beautiful, especially the Oriental lilies from Korea and Japan. I often arrange them in tall bottles of different sizes, shapes, and colors that I collect on my travels to Europe. I also collect various baskets as containers for my plants. I think that a plant looks more dressed up when it's set inside a basket. I often put a vase of roses on a table with lilies or with an orchid plant. An amaryllis next to a

DARK PURPLE,
RED, WHITE DAHLIA

130

hydrangea is quite pretty, as well as an amaryllis with a geranium. The height of the amaryllis makes it a choice companion in an arrangement, especially with rather short, bushy plants. Or try an amaryllis in a basket with lilies of the valley around it. They come in lovely shades of red, white, pink, and even orange. In your arrangements, as well as contrasting and matching colors, you can contrast and match sizes and shapes. That is what I do, and the combinations are dazzling. Clivia plants, which are bulbs, are another favorite of mine. They are a spectacular orange color and make a very impressive showing on any table. Clivia plants come from Borneo, so they are fairly difficult to find, but if you ever have the chance to buy one, do, and you'll never be sorry. For your lunches or dinner parties I suggest a low cut flower or plant—maybe even an orchid—so that you can see across the table.

Discovering New Arrangements

As I have said, you can let your imagination run wild. Last week I discovered a fabulous new arrangement for one room in my house by placing some of the new Envy zinnias in two K'ang Hsi frogs (Chinese porcelain) at each end of a coffee table. In the center I put a tall cattleya orchid. The Envy zinnias are a lovely light green and the cattleya is pale lavender with a yellow throat —together they are exquisite! I then put several more orchids of the same color on the other tables in the room and then added yellow zinnias in vases. To my surprise, the effect was spectacular!

PINK PEONY

131

And I had great fun creating it. If you have an outdoor patio, potted geraniums, hydrangeas, daisies, or jasmine can be a gay addition. Some people like roses in pots. Even miniatures are pretty. I suggest dwarf fruit trees, which I think look the prettiest in wooden tubs. For the bedroom I prefer roses in a vase or a few small orchid plants, but a bouquet of violets is the best. For my front hall I like big plants in baskets, such as tall lilies. Some species of orchids, such as cymbidiums, grow quite tall, and I use them as I do the lilies, lemon trees, and camellia bushes. Also standard geraniums and standard white or pink azaleas. All of these, naturally, must be in season. Maybe you could use one or all of them to make your entrance hall pretty. When I walk into someone's house and see beautiful flowers, it automatically puts me in a good mood. I think it really tells something about the people. After all, it does take some care and trouble to put them there. Why don't you try bringing plants and flowers into your Life? You will be surprised at the difference they make.

The thrill of springtime exists for everyone. I always feel sorry for those who are forced to miss it. I am so excited to see the bulbs I planted last fall pushing their noses out of the ground. Every day is a new surprise—different species of birds arriving, fighting for their different territories. Even pheasants appear on my place, crowing for their mates. And those darling little chipmunks coming out of their burrows, awakening at the call of spring. Most of us have no idea how busy

I have no set rules for designing arrangements. I love all flowers, separately or mixed together, and I find that most flowers complement one another. This bouquet of roses from my cutting garden is not only beautiful but it will keep my home smelling sweet.

Yellow Chinese Tree Peonies (opposite) are among my favorite flowers—they are almost too beautiful for words!

Another long-lasting and fragrant cut flower is the peony (left), a perennial that also has a long life in a garden.

These perennial flowers bloom at different times during the season: Peonies blossom in late May or early June and lilies in July, August, and September. These lilies, known as 'Yellow Blaze' Asiatic Hybrids (above), are both breathtaking and also last as cut flowers for two or three weeks.

If properly cared for, peonies can easily survive for half a century in the garden. The real key to making peonies bloom is the planting depth—your best bet is to lay a stick across the hole and measure two inches from the soil line to the bud tips.

Mother Earth is at this time, releasing all her family. It's almost like magic! Think how exciting the first warm day is—to hear one bird—the smell in the air—to run outside barefoot—to lie in the grass—there is electricity in the air and it is transferred to us! The renewal of life. Everything we have the earth gives us—we take it so for granted. Don't let yourself miss this. Gardening is the best therapy in the world. You can put so much into it and get so much back. Love is everything. . . . How lucky we are to live on this beautiful earth—you can bring the beauty to yourselves through gardening. Your garden will help you realize and appreciate how truly exquisite nature is!

C. Z. Guest
"Templeton," Old Westbury, Long Island, New York

C. Z. Guest

Author of the text, C. Z. Guest was Commissioner General of the American Exhibit at the 1984 International Garden Festival in Liverpool, England. A leader of society and an exceptional horsewoman, she has recently entered the fashion business, designing a signature line of sportswear. She writes a gardening column for 12 newspapers, including the *New York Post,* the *Boston Herald,* and the *Chicago Sun-Times*.

Cecil Beaton

The contributor of the original drawings reproduced in this book, Mr. Beaton is perhaps best known for his photographic portraits of Britain's royal family. He was also a writer, set and costume designer, and painter. Mr. Beaton won an Oscar for costume design for the film *Gigi,* and an Antoinette Perry Award for the musical *My Fair Lady*. He has published several books, including collections of photographs and personal diaries. Mr. Beaton travelled extensively, but made his home in England. He died in 1980.

Truman Capote

Included in this book is an introduction by Truman Capote, one of the major American writers of the second half of this century. A self-proclaimed "stylist," he wrote 13 books, including novels, short stories, and dramatizations. He is also the author of *In Cold Blood, Breakfast at Tiffany's, Other Voices, Other Rooms,* and *A Tree of Night*. He died in 1984.

Elvin McDonald

The photographer of C. Z. Guest's gardens, Mr. McDonald is a noted garden authority in his own right. He has written more than 40 books on plants and gardening. He was formerly the Garden Editor of *House Beautiful* and Garden Consultant for *Family Circle,* and has also established his own gardening newsletter. His syndicated columns appear biweekly in 150 newspapers. Mr. McDonald is on the editorial board of *Garden Design Magazine* and The Garden Book Club and is director of Special Projects at the Brooklyn Botanic Gardens.

CRIMSON
ROSE

The plant hardiness zone map—devised by the United States Department of Agriculture—is used in countless nursery catalogs and garden books to indicate where plants can be grown.

In the map's original concept, the reader was to locate on the map the climate zone in which he lived; then, if the zone number given for a particular plant was the same as, or smaller than, his climate zone number, the plant was judged to be hardy in his locale.

In our listings, we have followed the standard method of hardiness rating; but in addition to indicating the coldest zone the plant will grow in, we consider its adaptability and usefulness in the warmer zones, and indicate all zones in which the plant is generally grown.

The limitations of the map are obvious. It is impossible to accurately map local variations in climate.

Furthermore, a map based on temperatures only is misleading when considering plants which have special soil requirements; for example, plants such as rhododendrons and pieris require acid soil, but this soil will not necessarily be found throughout their range of favorable growing climates.

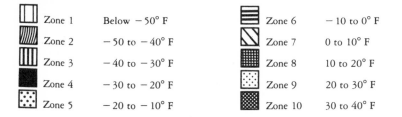
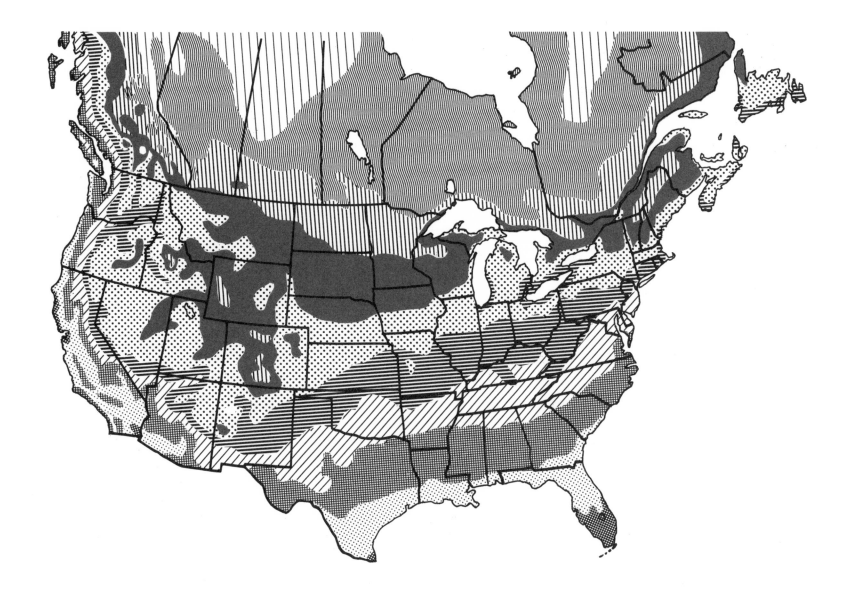

Index

Numbers in italics indicate
  photographs